The Pussy's Tail
and other poems

Dedicated to the children to whom I read my poems and
who rewarded me with their laughter.

The Pussy's Tail

and other poems

Ernest Yelf

*For Emily,
With best wishes
Ernt E. Yelf 8.11.'04*

Owlprint

Published in 2004 by

Owlprint
PO9 3HE 7

Copyright © Ernest Yelf, 2004.

The moral right of the author has been asserted.

All rights reserved. Without limiting the rights under copyright reserved above, no part of this publication may be reproduced, stored or introduced into a retrieval system, or transmitted, in any form or by any means (electronic, mechanical, photocopying, recording or otherwise), without the prior written permission of the copyright owner and author of this book.

ISBN No 0-9548722-0-7

A catalogue record of this book can be obtained from the British Library

Illustrations by Ian Tyrrell © 2004

Printed and bound in Great Britain by
RPM Print & Design
Chichester, West Sussex

Contents

	Page
Introduction	vii
A Cautionary Tale For Noisy Children	1
The Missing Link	6
My Valentine	8
Noses	10
The Worm Who Turned	11
Legs	17
Veterinary Practice	18
Frobbits	20
The Owl Who Didn't Give A Hoot	21
Number Puzzle	27
The Mousetronaut	28
The Pyjama Fruit	32
Ears	33
Flower Pott, Buttercup, Raspberry And Wendy	35
Burning Bright	38
A Fishy Tale	39
Life Goes On Its Way	40
Emily Porter	43
Geometry Set	46
Christmas Eve 1	48
The Little Man	49
Fatima's Round	52
An Ill Wind	54
Christmas Eve 2	57
The Pussy's Tale	59
The Time Machine	67
Hippopotamus	68
The Message	69
The End	70

INTRODUCTION

This small collection of poems primarily is intended for children but it is my hope that they may be enjoyed by all from seven to ninety seven who have carried into adulthood that particular childhood ability to laugh at the nonsensical.

A Cautionary Tale For Noisy Children and The Missing Link were written for a specific primary class, year three, in 2001 and 2002 respectively; they were never intended for any purpose other than the enjoyment of the children at the time and are included only as representing the 'beginning'. A Cautionary Tale For Noisy Children is nothing more than an assertive limerick that grew too big for its boots and was unable to contain itself within four lines. The Missing Link concerns a condition that will be recognised by all teachers: I have endeavoured to present it in such manner as to minimise the stress of discovering that the subject has intruded into a rare moment of relaxation during which the poem may be read.

As a child, the singular 'Cautionary Tales' of Hilaire Belloc kindled affection for darker humour which, as a teenager, blended with the inspired nonsense of Spike Milligan and in later years the extraordinary 'Revolting Rhymes' of Roald Dahl. The impression created by such verses is indelible and if their influence is perceived in the following pages, I offer no apology.

Ernest Yelf.   August 2004

A Cautionary Tale For Noisy Children

Mrs. Wood is a very fine teacher,
Her teaching is skilful and calm,
But the story that I'm going to tell you,
Could cause you no little alarm.

For teaching a class can be stressful
And stress can cause changes in folk,
So think twice before next you are noisy,
For Mrs. Wood's change was no joke.

When the noise reached a painful crescendo,
She slipped out for an aspirin or two,
She was only away for five minutes,
With an outcome surprising but true.

When soothing her headache with aspirin,
She discovered with shock and dismay,
The classroom was silent and empty,
Year Three all had tiptoed away.

Through the window she heard in the distance
The cry "we are free, we are free,"
An alarming transmogrification
Overcame Mrs. Wood as we'll see.

Her eyes turned a luminous purple,
Her bright scarlet 'lippy' turned green,
The transition was really quite shocking
And by children should never be seen.

Mrs. Wood was quite proud of her eyeballs,
An unusual and beautiful green,
The left one was kept in a jar by the bed,
Popped in every night for a clean.

So the change in this prominent feature,
Occasioned by Year three absconding,
Has caused quite irreparable damage
To the progress of child/teacher bonding.

Her blond hair turned all black and crinkly,
Her nose grew too big for her face,
From the cupboard she took out a broomstick
And flew off to give the class chase.

As I've said Mrs. Wood's a fine teacher
But where flying of brooms is concerned,
Well, her skills are a little bit 'iffy',
There are lessons she never has learned.

She could fly the broom only in circles,
She never knew how to fly straight
And it's said if you travel in circles,
You may suffer a terrible fate.

As she flew round the school like a rocket,
Mrs. Mullen turned blue in the face;
"To lose two or three is forgivable
But a whole class? A total disgrace!"

"Bring them back or you'll go in detention,
I'll hide all your lipsticky stock,"
Then her hair went all spiky and upwards,
Like a hedgehog whose had a bad shock.

When the children discovered what happened,
It caused them considerable mirth,
Mrs. Wood was last seen over Scotland,
Some say that she circled the earth.

Year Three were all found in McDonalds,
Mrs. Wood? Well, she came to no harm
But she did lose control of her broomstick
And crashed (*the poor thing*) on Budd's Farm.

The pong was truly appalling
But most of it's now gone away,
Apart from in really hot weather,
When a whiff is determined to stay.

In bed, before dawn, at a quarter to four,
Mrs. Wood had a fright and fell on to the floor,
She sat bolt upright and started to scream,
The escape of Year Three was a terrible dream.

Truth can be stranger than fiction,
With you these wise words I will share;
The other day when I was leaving,
Were those bristles I saw on her chair?

No, surely not, it's a trick of the light,
Some nightmares must never come true,
We hold in our hands our own future
And your future's all up to you.

To be certain she'll stay as you see her today
Remember this one golden rule;
Fun and noise must be saved for the playground,
Lessons are learned when in school.

The Missing Link

Now Miss Newman's in charge of Year Three!
With long curling tresses and suitable dresses
All seeing 'specs' and guitar,
She's determined the children will learn and progress
So in life they'll succeed and go far;
But a problem exists, as all good teachers know,
Of a curious incomplete link,
Between ears and the brain of the dear little things
And reluctance at times just to think.

The division of twelve by the unit of three,
The answer we all know is four,
The inverse is simple and often is taught,
That three fours are twelve and no more;
But should we discourage original thought
That says three lots of four are sixteen,
So unselfish an answer, such a generous sum,
Would not marking it wrong be thought mean?
Think of Einstein and Newton, unconstrained minds
With no teacher to guide and restrict them;
Sigmund Freud is my preference, he'd blame it on dreams
But they're not in the National Curriculum.

So Miss Newman's in charge of Year Three,
Yes Miss Newman's in charge of Year Three
And cerebral nourishment's gently applied
To fill all the nooks and the crannies inside
Those little grey cells, with minimum pain,
To restore the lost link between ears and the brain.

Lessons are over, brainboxes swell,
Year Three all line up at the sound of the bell;
There's Emma and Jamie, Harry and Nardia,
Elliott and Emily J,
Connor and Christian, Coran and Connie,
Steven and Emily A,
Lewis and James, Alex and George,
Thomas W, Alison D,
Thomas E and Georgina, Stephanie, Nicola,
Lawrence and Matthew G,
Daisy, Harry and Edward, Luke Jade and Ashlea,
Matthew L and not least Matthew B,
All bursting with knowledge, connection achieved,
At 3.35 Miss Newman's relieved;
They worked really hard, all they've learnt, to retain,
But next morning we start all over again!

My Valentine

"I love you little sausage,"
Words you seldom hear,
Except on February the fourteenth,
A soppy time of year.
The day belongs to Valentine
The patron saint of lovers,
He's to blame for names like this
And quite a lot of others
Like, Gooseberry and Rabbit Face,
Cuddle Buns and Sprout,
Pea and Prune and Piggy Poohs,
I've left the worst ones out.
Who cares about St. Valentine,
There are many other days
When we can say, "I love you,"
In our funny, different ways.

So, "I love you little sausage,"
Keen as mustard as they say,
The English one of course,
The one that takes your breath away.
"I could eat you little sausage,"
As you lie upon your bed
Of steaming mashed potato,
No more need be said
Except, "I miss you little sausage,"
Now that you have gone
But there's a 'two for one' at Waitrose
So I won't miss you for long!

Noses

The nose is an embarrassment,
It stands up on your face,
Points (*and we all know that's rude*),
You would think it owned the place.
Underneath are two black holes,
Some are much too wide,
Don't ever put your finger in,
There are nasty things inside.
I know they are for sniffing,
But why does it need two?
Because the nose is just a show off,
It's quite clear one will do.
If one is all that's needed
It might as well be flat;
The conclusion is its useless,
So that's enough of that.

The Worm Who Turned

There was a lazy little worm
Whose lessons he would never learn,
In class he'd snooze and pick his nose
And wonder why he had no toes
And other such time wasting thoughts
Like, why don't elephants wear shorts?
A pachyderm's enormous bottom
Wearing crisp, white, shining cotton,
Amused the little worm a lot,
But added not a single jot
To knowledge of division,
Or tables, in fact all of maths
He treated with derision.
Why should he learn this stupid stuff?
This worm declared, he'd had enough.

So Ernie, yes that was his name,
Was hatching in his little brain
A plot that was not very kind
To his poor teachers peace of mind.
He would stand up on his pointy end,
As high as he could measure,
Fill himself with wind and then
Release it under pressure.
After gaining her attention
With this quite disgusting ploy,

He'd shout out his appalling maths,
To more than just annoy.

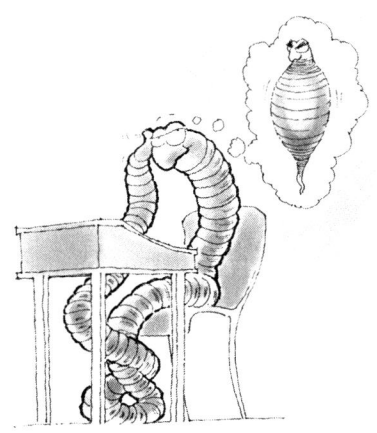

For if each day his dismal
Mathematics skills he showed,
Eventually, he was quite sure,
His teacher would explode.
The last sum he would ever do,
And this had Ern in fits,
Was to wriggle round the classroom
Counting all the bits.
Some would say it's 'wormist'
To imply that worms aren't bright
But Ernie is the living proof,
He never sees the light.
Alas his plan to undermine
His teacher's numerology,

Was doomed by over confidence
In feeble worm-psychology.
She was devoted to the theory,
Few considered sound,
That even worms have prospects,
If helped out of the ground
But in plotting her removal
He had failed to grasp at all
That she was very, very strict
And very, very tall.

It's sometimes sound advice to see
Ourselves as others do,
Ernie had not done this,
A mistake that he would rue.
Her humour was extinguished
By his startling first emission,
She would not stand for earthworms
In a vertical position,
But most of all to stop
That squeaky, squirmy, wormy voice,
Insulting her beloved maths,
She really had no choice.

This innumerate invertebrate,
Will, if teacher's law prevails,
 Become instant 'earthworm paté'
(*Well why not? The French eat snails*).

Ernie was perplexed to find
His teacher still intact,
The explosion he had plotted,
Had not become a fact.
With chest thrust forth and
Eyes ablaze, a luminescent green,
This was an aspect of his teacher
The worm had never seen.
A mighty bellow rent the air
But Ernie still was at a loss,
To understand her body language
Signalled slightly more than cross,
Until a shadow fell upon him,
Cast by a giant foot,
Instant change of plan he thought,
Or this worm will be 'caput'
"An Isosceles Trapezium
Has two sides with lengths the same
But only those non-parallel,
Or it wouldn't have this name."
Suffice to say that what it meant,
He didn't have a clue,
From deep in his subconscious
This forgotten maths he drew.
The foot stopped from his squirmy frame,
A whisker at the most,
He was saved from being spread upon
His teacher's tea time toast.

Some conclusions are confounding
And much to my surprise,
Both Ernie and his teacher
Received a Nobel Prize.
For her thesis on worm flatulence
She became the major player,
In exploiting this new power source,
That saved the Ozone Layer.

Ernie owns a Wind Farm,
Employing ninety million worms,
Providing gas for heating
Big multinational firms.

From his teacher he discovered
The skill of being strict,
So worms whose wind is underpowered,
Off they will be ticked.
This fable now is at an end,
The drama is concluded,
If you found a moral in this verse
You're welcome, but deluded.
Just rejoice in this unlikely tale
Of reconciliation,
Between a teacher and a little worm
Who hated numeration.

Legs

Legs are very useful things
That hang down from our bottom,
For running and for walking,
We should be jolly glad we've 'gottem'.
The fact that they move back and forth,
Is a really good invention,
Put the right one next to left
And then you're standing to attention.
The bendy bit that's half way up,
Known commonly as knee,
Allows us to sit down and rest
And have a cup of tea.
So the next time you are pestering
Your parents for a lift,
Don't be lazy, use your legs instead,
They're evolution's clever gift.

Veterinary Practice

My doggie has a headache,
I was unaware until,
The vet told me he had one
And then sent me the bill.

My guinea pig's left handed,
I was unaware until,
The vet advised me that it was
And then sent me the bill.

My goldfish has amnesia,
I was unaware until,
The vet discovered it was so
And then sent me the bill.

My parrot is religious,
I was unaware until,
The vet assured me it was true
And then sent me the bill.

My tortoise only has three legs,
I was quite aware but still,
The vet confirmed the handicap
And then sent me the bill.

My vet he has a headache,
I was unaware until,
He was summoned by the magistrates;
Now he must pay the bill!

Frobbits

Even in the darkest wood,
A Frobbit's very rare,
If you think you've seen one,
It was probably not there.
No photographs exist,
There are none in any zoo,
I'm the only one who's seen them,
Now I'm pleased that you have too.
They're in your imagination,
They hopped in there from mine,
They won't look the same, I know
But when we meet next time,
We'll compare our little Frobbits,
Quite soon we'll have to share,
When lots have read this poem,
There'll be Frobbits everywhere!

The Owl Who Didn't Give A Hoot

The owl is a majestic bird,
Dignified and wise,
Surveying all around him
Through his big, black, owlish eyes.
He is the Woodland Magistrate,
Elected by his peers,
For his accumulated wisdom,
Over many woodland years.
His impressive lineage,
Is held in high regard,
By all the woodland creatures,
So it's really rather hard
To tell the tale of Ollie,
An owl of ill repute,
Whose very bad behaviour showed,
He didn't 'give a hoot'.
He runs along the branches,
Although he knows that he should walk,
Tail feathers always hanging out
And you should hear him talk;
'To wit'; 'to wit'; 'to wit' he cries,
Just to contradict the view,
That any self respecting owl
Would cry, 'To wit, to woo'.

A holidaying bullfrog
Was snoozing by a stream,
Unsuspecting that the little owl,
Was about to spoil his dream.
"Hop off," screamed the horrid owl,
"Woof, woof," replied the frog,
So startled by his odd response,
He fell backward off his log.
Long, pink, pointed nostrils,
Sniffed out of a hole,
"Get lost", screamed the naughty owl,
To a disconcerted mole.
"Woof, woof," the tiny mole replied
And promptly had a fit,
He loved his little moley voice
And "woof, woof," was not it.

Confidence deflated,
He crept back down his hole,
How could he ever find a girlfriend,
Who would love a 'barking mole'?

The mental cruelty inflicted
On these small, defenceless creatures,
Alas, was not the worst of Ollie's
Anti social features.
I cannot use the language
Which is called for to convey,
The horrors he inflicted on
That fateful summers day.
As children, from experience,
There is no doubt in my mind,
You will guess at once what Ollie did,
Despite my words refined.

The Long Legs wander in the woods
At weekends, to relax,
They sometimes come with Little Legs
And picnics on their backs,
Although not feathered creatures,
The owls consider them as friends
And discourage owl behaviour,
Which in any way offends.

One such Long Leg family,
Laid out their picnic tea,
As fate decreed they chose to sit,
Right under Ollie's tree.
Ollie is a frequent diner
At 'To Wittie's Curry House'
Last night, fit to burst,
He stuffed himself with curried mouse.
So, in a sense, he joined their picnic,
Though not at their request,
The fact he stayed upon his branch,
His contribution can be guessed.
The Long Legs ran for cover,
For, though Delia Smith may try,
Curried mouse does not improve
The taste of apple pie.

'Hooticulture' had been desecrated,
The owls would take no more,
Long Legs in bad odour,
Was the final, final straw.
The 'Owlternet' was twittering,
The Wise Owl Council was recalled,
With two or three exceptions,
The Wise Owls were appalled.
The progressives said, "Just let him be,
Why suppress his creativity?"
 But wisdom and good sense prevailed,

Owlcentred learning, long had failed.
Something will be done about,
At last there's no dispute,
The behaviour of the little owl,
Who did not 'give a hoot'.

Before justice was administered,
A strange event occurred,
Which changed the bad behaviour
Of the disrespectful bird.
His following of little owls,
Who had laughed and cheered him on,
After Long Legs were humiliated,
Suddenly had gone.
What is the point of clowning
When the circus tent has emptied?
From that moment on the little owl,
Regretted and repented.

As yet this page cannot be closed,
There are further revelations,
The woofing frog, the barking mole,
Are unresolved sensations.
Oliver's embarrassed,
But I have taken the decision,
To tell you of the book
From which he learned, ventriloquism.

These events were many years ago,
He recalls with misty eyes,
Now he leads the Wise Owl Council,
He is Oliver the Wise
But a tiny piece of Ollie still remains
Deep down inside,
As in certain grown up Long Legs,
Childhood spirit still resides;
Each Friday night accompanied,
By his pretty tawny spouse,
He dines out at 'To Wittie's',
On his favourite Curried Mouse.

Number Puzzle

Be gentle Mrs. Olive-Jones
My brain is rather tired,
I've tried to understand
But my attention span's expired;
You explained it very carefully,
You wrote it on the board
And not a word you said have I
Deliberately ignored.
I've made a special effort
So my sums look really neat,
Each digit in a separate square
And every sum complete
By underlining, with a ruler,
With a line that's not too long;
The only thing that spoils them
Is that, every answer's wrong.
I know I can do better
So when I've had a good nights rest
And we start again tomorrow
I'll try my very, very best.
Sums are easy for a teacher,
For you they're fundamental
But I am only eight years old
So, Mrs. Olive-Jones, be gentle.

The Mousetronaut

An elephant is very large,
A mouse is very small,
If the one treads on the other,
There would be no mouse at all.
However, size is unimportant,
When considering survival,
For speed and nimbleness of foot,
The mouse has no close rival.
It is another matter
To deliberately provoke,
An enormous, grumpy elephant,
He may not see the joke,
Especially when he's sleeping,
He is not at his best,
To appreciate the humour
Of a little mouse's jest.

In his very best pyjamas,
The elephant is snoring,
The moment when the mouse decided,
He would go exploring;
Heroic mice seek bigger holes,
Deep and dark and cosy,
But this hole was a big mistake,
He would pay for being nosy.

Picked up some unidentified
And quite unearthly cries.
They put it down to interference,
From the Asteroidal Belt
But I am certain that the sound
Could be interpreted as "heeelp"!

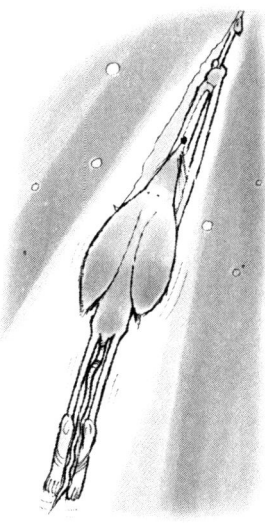

The mouse was never seen again
But do not be distraught,
It's possible that he may be,
Much closer than we thought.
When you hear reports of UFOs
And aliens from space,
Just wonder why they always have,
That strangely, mousey face.

The Pyjama Fruit

There is a very special fruit,
Alas, we take for granted,
It is without a single doubt,
The best that nature planted.

It gives you lots of energy,
Far greater than most tonics
But few know that its shape results,
From nature's ergonomics.

That's why it's like a handle,
So comfortable for holding,
Stuff one in your pocket
And its thick skin stops it folding.

When next you plan a midnight feast,
In your yellow striped pyjamas,
Choose the fruits that match (and rhyme),
So bedtime means Bananas!

Ears

The flappy, sticky-outy things,
On each side of our head,
Have many uses other than,
For hearing what is said.
For those of us whose eyesight,
Is not quite what it should be,
They prevent our specs from dropping off
And floating out to sea,
They stop our hats from slipping down
And covering our eyes
And if we flap them fast enough,
They drive away the flies.
Really, really big ones,
Can shade us from the sun
And painting them bright yellow,
For your teacher can be fun.

If you think they're not appreciated,
Light them up at night,
Run into your parents' room
And see if they take fright.
With an awful lot of practice,
But I have heard it's worth a try
For those with giant whoppers,
You can leave the ground and fly.

If you want them to do all these things,
Here is a special warning,
You must clean them out before
You go to bed and in the morning.
If you do they'll go on working,
For years and years and years,
So keep them washed and polished
And shout out, 'three cheers for ears'!

Poet's Note:
This poem can be read at a steadily increasing speed.

Flower Pott, Buttercup, Raspberry and Wendy

Flower Pott, I promise you, Flower Pott they called her;
When Flower reached the age of understanding, it appalled her.
Flower's just about acceptable but definitely not,
When followed by a surname as unfortunate as Pott.
The Potts were not the brightest and it's clear they had not known,
By naming Flower, Flower, they would reap what they had sown.

Such insensitive indulgence had left other children fuming
At their parents sense of humour or for selfishly assuming
That by making them the subject of a rather silly pun,
They would not be tormented by what others thought was fun.
When she was fast asleep she stuck her bottom in the air,
So her parents called her Buttercup, without a thought or care
For the teasing she would suffer, it frequently occurs,
Buttercup had sworn revenge; the last laugh would be hers.
Raspberry was angry at the sentiments conveyed,
When first they saw their little fruit, that was the noise they made.
It's true the child was spotty but they disappear in time,
Unlike the dreadful name they chose, a truly shocking crime.
It will not go unpunished, as Raspberry declared,
Her parents will be sentenced to humiliation shared.
Wendy, you'll be thinking, is a name that's rather pretty,
Its inclusion is mistaken or at best an awful pity;
It was the parent's favourite name it gave them untold joy
But they were both short-sighted; their offspring was a boy.

It really is not funny when you grow up tall and hairy,
To answer to a name that's more in keeping with a fairy
And despite a certain tragedy in this final name,
Myopia is no excuse for causing so much pain.
When Wendy (*at the age of ten unusually matured*)
Was shaving twice a week it made much worse what he endured.
The image in the mirror had stirred him into action,
For the torture they had caused, he'd drive his parents to distraction.

Flower Pott, Buttercup, Raspberry and Wendy,
Were neighbours in a cul-de-sac their parents thought was trendy.
Each week they shopped at Waitrose, they imagined it was posh
And spent enormous sums of money on unnecessary 'nosh'.
They gathered by their favourite spot, the counter selling cheeses,
To loudly air their knowledge of varieties of 'Brieses'.
This parents' club for showing off, to children a disgrace,
As the scene of final reckoning, it had to be the place.
At eleven on a Saturday the children planned to strike,
All were wearing football boots and one was on a bike,
Dashing by the shoppers, the next bit's rather rude,
For maximum embarrassment, all four were in the nude.
Shouting out their parents' names they mounted the attack,
As they leapt into the cheese display, there was no turning back;
They jumped upon, danced upon, rode upon the stock,
Sending Wensleydale and Camembert whizzing round the shop;
The parents stood with open mouths, their faces growing redder,
Frozen to the spot amongst the flying Brie and Cheddar,
The Stiltons and the Lancashire, much flatter that was planned

And Cheshire cheese with tyre marks distinctly second-hand.
Gorgonzola is a special cheese famous for its 'humming'
But Mrs. Pott was so upset she did not see it coming.
Her sense of smell had warned her of its imminent arrival,
Alas, too late to guarantee Mrs. Pott's survival.
Like a meteor approaching its progress never slows,
She no longer needed sense of smell, the cheese was up her nose!

Despite our disapproval of such very bad behaviour,
The children's retribution is a memory to savour.
The four of them were heroes, at least amongst their peers,
No more were they ridiculed throughout their growing years
And as each of them was under age, their parents took the blame,
Whose reputation in the cul-de-sac was never quite the same again.
The battle of the cheeses over years has well matured,
To which a curious statistic, a sort of legacy, endured;
Never in the history of cheese and things like that,
Have so many reached their 'sell by' date in sixty seconds flat.

'Burning Bright'

In the presence of a tiger,
Remain dignified and calm;
Most important, never fall,
For deadly tiger charm.
His captivating tiger smile,
Which seems to say, "my friend,"
Does not necessarily,
Show what he may intend.
By now he will be close enough,
For you to see what lies beneath;
Two rows of healthy, glistening,
Razor sharp, white teeth.
His burning, opal, tiger eyes,
Arouse in you a glimmer
Of realisation that his steady gaze,
Is looking at his dinner.
His carnivorous charisma,
Has devoured your fickle fate,
The tiger's smile is now a grin;
It was not all the tiger ate.

Poet's Note:
Dedicated to a good friend who stood close
enough for me to write this poem from a safe distance.

A Fishy Tale

The sardine is adaptable,
It has no use for fins,
You fish for them with magnets,
Because sardines live in tins.

Life Goes On Its Way

By an ancient woodland path, many years ago,
A tiny mushroom fretted as his growth was much too slow.
His vertical proportions were only half the size
Of other mushrooms in the wood, despite constant exercise.
He made himself a mushroom hat, it made him look much taller,
But his fellow mushrooms sniggered, his self esteem was even smaller.
At this point, I fully understand, there will be those among us,
Who will find it very hard to show compassion for a fungus
But there are others we have yet to meet whose lives are intertwined,
So have patience with the mushroom and don't be so unkind.

The wizened, weary woodsman trudges on his weary way,
To his task of endless chopping through another weary day.
He has an aged and wrinkled face of which poets eulogise
But it's not through age and wisdom that he has two large black eyes.
Each morning at the crack of dawn his footsteps can be heard,

With cursing and much louder, a very vulgar word
But we must be tolerant for as the woodsman passes,
He keeps bumping into trees as no one's yet invented glasses.
Looming through the morning mist a spectre plods its course,
This bony apparition long ago looked like a horse;
The woodsman feeds it Brussels sprouts and works it much too hard,
He paid two pennies for the creature from a local knackers yard.
The nag, though frail, is clever though it has still not understood
The reason for the woodsman's violent progress through the wood
But it relishes a moment's rest and as the woodsman bumps and howls,
It pursues its only joy in life, it opens up its bowels!

It was sometime before the mushroom once again would see the light,
The darkness that descended from above turned day to night.
This answer to a mushroom's prayer, this spontaneous act of horse,
Transformed the mushroom's stature and its future changed its course.
Inflated by its sudden growth the mushroom swayed and swaggered,
Few things are more annoying than a mushroom who's a braggart.
Its behaviour was embarrassing, no self respect at all
But even in the mushroom world pride comes before a fall.
The wizened, weary woodsman trudges on his weary way,
To his task of endless chopping through another weary day.
He tripped up on a chestnut root, fell cursing to the ground
But on opening his two black eyes, was moved by what he found.
An unfamiliar creaking sound spread across his face,
As the corners of his mouth went up and put a smile in place.
"That's meant for me," the woodsman choked, "at last I'm not forsaken,"
"That juicy, giant mushroom will go well with eggs and bacon."

He chopped it down, took it home, sliced it, fried and eat it,
The mushroom's purpose now was served, it's best if we forget it.
The horse had had its moment; the mushroom had its day;
The woodsman found a cause to smile and life goes on its way.

Emily Porter

A charming young lady named Emily Porter,
Did everything her caring parents had taught her;
She'd not speak when her mouth was still half full of food
And interrupting when someone was talking, was rude;
She would hold open doors and say thank you and please,
Her impeccable manners, she practised with ease.
The impression she fostered of female perfection,
Was betrayed by a hobby immune to correction,
For this foolish young lady, Miss Emily Porter,
Delighted in jumping in puddles of water.
The bigger the puddle the larger the splashing
And if someone was soaked it was doubly smashing.
Her parents had warned her it would all end in tears
But Emily simply compounded their fears.
Her persistence, we know, was misguided and wilful
But you had to admit, she became rather skilful;
When her feet hit the puddle the violent connection,
Sent water cascading in every direction.
Her dumfounded victims, soaked by the waters,
Were further enraged when Emily Porter's
Angelic smile and fluttering lashes,
Were followed by further deliberate splashes.
The fifteenth of October, the night of the storm,
Emily's tucked up all cosy and warm.
Good children, of course, all are sleeping and dreaming
But Emily's wide awake busily scheming.

The volume of water descending to earth,
Would provide her with hours of mischief and mirth.
This was the moment at which fate decided,
Her planning and premature end, coincided.
The next morning, as fast as good manners enable,
She finished her breakfast and then cleared the table,
Brushed her hair, cleaned her teeth, as all children should
And promised her mother that she would be good.
It's wicked to promise when you know it's a token,
By the time she left home hers was already broken.

Within moments she saw it, as big as a lake,
Well not quite but a large one make no mistake,
It was next to a bus stop, perfectly placed,
To drench the whole bus queue a chance not to waste.
With both feet together she flew through the air,
Her technique perfected her aim fair and square,
The water cascaded now the moment we feared,
In the blink of an eye the poor girl disappeared.
As she had been warned, it would all end in pain,
For this was no puddle but an uncovered drain.
If only the words of her elders she'd heeded,
This tragic conclusion would not have been needed.
I'm aware it's distressing but there's no use pretending,
In life, not all stories have the happiest ending.
The bubbles that rose from the very deep water,
Were the last that was seen of Miss Emily Porter.

Poet's Note:
If another Emily Porter reads this poem I'm sure you are
a very nice person who wouldn't splash people like this.

Geometry Set

The octagon was lonely,
He was looking for a mate,
To appreciate his symmetry
And impressive set of eight.

He met a quadrilateral,
She was only half his size
But the octagon was smitten,
He could not avert his eyes.

She only had four angles,
He really did not care,
With her double, double vertices,
She was a perfect square.

The little square was puzzled
By the octagon's attentions,
Her shape was plain, her sides were straight,
With very small dimensions.

She learned they shared a family tree
With many sided branches,
Now she knew they both were polygons,
She welcomed his advances.

The octagon and little square
Both had the same intention,
Their life, a rather flat affair,
Would gain a third dimension.

The outcome of their geometry,
The story is complete,
Eight perfect polyhedra,
Each with eight, flat little feet.

Christmas Eve – 1

The moon is bright at midnight,
Snow is on the ground,
The countryside is silent,
Except the distant sound
Of church bells in the crisp night air,
Inviting all to pray,
This is a very special night,
Tomorrow's Christmas Day.
Rabbits snug in warrens,
Little mice in mousey holes,
As bells ring out to celebrate,
For me the church bell tolls.
A tear rolls down my wrinkled cheek,
I must prepare to leave,
As you rejoice, this is for me,
The final Christmas Eve.
Oh, I'll be there on Christmas Day,
Around about twelve thirty
But it won't be much fun for me,
As I'm the Christmas Turkey!

The Little Man

Sunrise on a lonely beach, extinguished ebbing night,
To contradict my solitude, a figure came in sight.
I'd swear that there was no one there a blink or so before,
When only I had owned the morning on this isolated shore.
Despite my disappointment at such selfish irritation,
I was determined not to stop and enter into conversation.
The figure was a little man dressed head to toe in green,
He really was the oddest little man I'd ever seen.
What was truly puzzling, to a strange encounter led,
The little man was upside down and standing on his head.
I pretended not to notice as I tried to hurry by
But I succumbed to curiosity and, unintended, caught his eye.
"Good day to you," he ventured, "Good morning," I replied,
As I failed to quell the urge to stop, no matter how I tried.
He said, "You think I am impertinent, I can tell it from your frown,
Forgive me, on this perfect day, why are you walking upside down?"
Few things are more infuriating when trying to relax,
Than an interfering little man who's contradicting facts.
With a growing sense of anger I replied, "Excuse me sir,
On this less than perfect morning from your words do I infer,
You are accusing *me* of acting in a manner unconventional,
When *your* misguided observation, to annoy, is quite intentional?"
His face resembled carrot juice, his pea green eyes were curious,
It was clear from his demeanour the little vegetable was furious.

"Well pardon me my observation, I assume this talk's bilateral,
Your method of progressing is inverted and unnatural."
At this I am ashamed to say I really blew my top;
It had not been an easy week, to my regret, I could not stop.
"You obnoxious, self opinionated, undernourished elf;
The only person upside down, your weedy little self."

I retreated, with my sharp response arousing in my mind,
A belated better judgement that my words had been unkind.
All the dignity compatible with marching off a shingle beach,
I summoned to say sorry for my rude, ill-tempered speech.

I turned to face the risen sun, now high above the shore,
To my surprise and consternation the little man was there no more.
Many times at dawn I walked again this lonely, magic place,
Now understanding my appearance to the upturned little face.
Whenever in my busy life I, with another, disagree,
The memory of the little man has enabled me to see,
The alternative opinion, I recommend that you do too;
The perspective will be different from the other's point of view.

Fatima's Round

Fatima the Belly Dancer,
Wobbled for a living;
Some were complimentary,
Others less forgiving.

Fatima's enthusiasm
Matched her 'cuddly' size,
Resulting in extraordinary
Sights before the eyes.

The wobble started at her top
And travelled to her bottom;
The bits that wobbled in between
Ideally are forgotten.

The Guinness Book of Records
Was her ultimate ambition,
To be the fastest Belly Dancer
From a standing start position.

Her confidence had over stretched
Her level of ability,
To keep control of all the parts
She moved with such agility.

Her dancing now was frenzied,
The wobbles far to fast;
Fatima was unaware
This dance would be her last.

A wobble going downward
Met a wobble coming back;
The result was loss of balance,
And really, that was that.

If you study Belly Dancing
There's a rule, you'll be aware,
That does *not* allow the dancer's legs
To stick up in the air.

This undignified departure,
A move she had not planned;
You'll never see her dance again,
Fatima was banned!

An Ill Wind

Arthur MacArthur of Scottish descent,
Played the bagpipes, unprompted, wherever he went.
His sense of what's tuneful and what is not,
Is a skill, if he ever possessed, he forgot.
He thought he played well but the evidence, sadly,
Is he plays on the bagpipes incredibly badly.
The bagpipes, at best, are a taste that's acquired,
Needing tolerant ears and playing inspired
But Arthur's attempts at the bag and the pipes,
Cause weakness and nausea, earache and fights.
The sound he created? well, think of a cat,
Whose tail is on fire, something like that
Only worse, a lot worse as this pained caterwauling
Was at ear splitting volume that was simply appalling.

His one claim to fame, which he mastered quite soon,
In ten seconds flat he could clear a large room.
It must not be inferred from these words, that they're 'snottish',
Of anything north of the border called Scottish.
Wrongly, of course, some think they are foreign
For inventing the haggis, the kilt and the sporran,
So in principle live and let live is just fine,
But when talking of bagpipes one must draw the line.
The damage that Arthur inflicted on trade
Just had to be stopped for each time he played,
Tourists in thousands scattered and fled
From the noise that could probably waken the dead.
Well it did but it cannot be told as I fear
There are details too grim for the innocent ear.
Desperate measures for the sake of the nation,
Amended the hunting with dogs' legislation.
A clause was inserted that permitted the sport
To pursue the MacArthur until he was caught.

Arthur was running, his little legs blurring,
Pursued by the hunters, a sight that was stirring
For those with a taste for the pack and the hunt,
Which does not include Arthur, because he's out in front.
The chase was unequal, now Arthur was certain,
His performing was over; he faced the last curtain.
There would be no encore, he'd at last come to learn
That his playing was hated, he would never return.
His final performance, it could not have been sadder,
He confronted the pack, inflated his bladder,

Stood to attention and started to play,
At the very first note every hound ran away.
The power of music from Arthur's perspective,
In saving his life had been very effective.
He escaped to the Highlands with a cave for his home,
Where he does little damage by his playing alone.
Now they flock in their thousands, to be first to have found,
The 'legendary beast' with the bloodcurdling sound.
So Arthur has triumphed, all thanks to the din
Of MacArthur, the piper, who would never give in.

Christmas Eve – 2

The moon is bright at midnight,
Snow is on the ground,
The countryside is silent,
Except the distant sound
Of church bells in the crisp night air,
Inviting all to pray,
This is a very special night,
Tomorrow's Christmas Day.
Moles in winter thermals,
Mice in mousey nest;
I've only frost and icicles,
To make my winter vest.
Rabbits snug in warrens,
Snuggling up as bunnies should;
Snowflakes are my overcoat,
In this freezing winter wood.
You'll think I am a spoilsport
But I'm afraid you must believe,
I'm delighted this will be my final
Outdoor, Christmas Eve.

They'll take me home tomorrow,
Put my feet into a pot,
Cover me in Christmas lights
And choose the perfect spot,
In the corner of the room,
Just as it should be,
So I'm the centre of attention
As befits, a Christmas Tree.

The Pussy's Tail

Morris was a ghastly child,
Who would drive his parents wild,
From a very early age,
By demanding with defiant rage,
From which they'd hide and calm each other
By pledging he'd not have a brother,
Or sister, come to that, they swore,
Enough's enough there'd be no more;
Although it was a sacrifice,
One little monster would suffice.
However, discipline is not a word
Of which his parents ever heard,
In fact, due to its total lack,
They made a rod for their own back;
Compounded by parental sin,
To his demands, they just gave in.

Morris would *not* be ignored;
He made a realistic sword,
Quite unsuitable for playing
But his parents just kept saying,
"Please be careful, never mind,
The vase you've broken, I'm sure we'll find
Another one that almost matches
And we'll hide the cuts and scratches

On the table legs with polish
But, to totally demolish
Grandma's favourite rocking chair,
When, clearly, she was sitting there,
Was that a teeny bit unfair?"
"There, there Morris, please don't scream,
You were told to in a dream?
So, Morris, as it wasn't you,
We'll mend the chair with super glue."
The silly parents should have said,
'Give us the sword and go to bed',
But their appeasement meant much faster,
Approached an even worse disaster.

The sword he'd used to such effect
In every detail was correct;
His skill in shaping wood and plastic,
Created something quite fantastic
And he was proud of what he'd made,
Especially as the sabre's blade
Would 'swish' when slicing through the air
And warnings that he must 'take care',
Untroubled him with grown-up fears
Of bruises, cuts and severed ears.
When you're young you're bold and fearless,
So what's so wrong with being earless,
You'd still have holes where sound goes in,
Who needs those useless bits of skin?
(*He would learn, the little twit,*
That those who plan to live by it,
With reasoning so badly flawed,
May perish by the homemade sword.)
The only problem to restrict him,
Where to find a willing victim
Happy to donate both ears,
To find one could take many years.
He had a brainwave, just like that,
He'd practice on his Grandma's cat.
Granny's eyesight's not so good,
At least one leg is made of wood.

He hid behind the kitchen door
And waited for the little paw,
As the unsuspecting cat,
Opened up the kitty flap,
Popped her head in, looked around,
What was that strangely swishing sound?

The cat shot in, the blade descended,
Results were not as he intended;
The cat let out a piercing wail,
Morris had cut off its, tail!
'Ouch', thought Morris, 'that's not funny',
'I could lose my pocket money';
The mercenary little beast
Showed no concern, not in the least,
For the pussy's state of mind,
Embarrassed by its bare behind.
Pussy was a modest creature,
Her tail had been her favourite feature,

No wonder she was going potty
Now everyone could see her botty.
Morris had one thought in mind,
That his Grandma should not find
The pussy's tail so what he'd do,
He'd stick it back with super glue.
He planned that he would hide until,
The wretched creature's standing still;
Despite his plan, he could not work it,
The cat now on its umpteenth circuit,
Unsurprisingly irate,
Was unwilling to co-operate.
Impatience now the catalyst,
Morris lunged and Morris missed;
Contact achieved but Morris froze,
He'd stuck the tail on pussy's nose.
The cat, already not amused,
Was, understandably, confused;
Her tail, apparently, was showing
Where the pussycat was going,
Contradicting nature's law,
That tails point where you've been before.
Her overloaded brain revolved
Around the odds that she'd evolved
Defensive features long forgotten;
She may have eyeballs in her bottom!
The cat was stuck, no way of knowing,
If she was coming, or she was going.

Meanwhile, Morris was distraught,
His surgery had come to naught
And he'd be 'for it' when he's found,
But then he heard a funny sound,
Approaching somewhere in the distance,
With a menacing persistence;
Three loud knocks and then a thud,
The sort of noise that chills the blood,
Especially as the sound grew near,
Morris was consumed with fear;
What was the sound, it's so uncanny?
The door flew open; it was Granny!
(*Two crutches and a wooden leg,*
A single woolly slipper,
Enough to scare the daylights,
From the petrified young nipper.)
It's odd, but when you least expect,
The little details you detect,
Like, Granny's eyes are red and glowing
And both her canine teeth are showing;
Her left-hand crutch, that's always there
Since falling from her rocking chair,
Is flying at you, through the air.
(*Though Granny's nearly ninety-eight*
And Morris only seven,
Developments have put in doubt
Who first may visit Heaven.)
Morris ducked and Morris fled,

The flying crutch hit puss instead.
Poor little moggie, so mistreated,
Her feline confidence depleted,
Victim of this family spat,
Is there no justice for a cat?

So Gran reclaimed her little kitty,
Admittedly not quite as pretty;
Confused and battered, frankly, weird,
Tailless, with a bushy beard
But Granny's eyes are rather weak
And when the pussy, so to speak,
Eventually departed for,
The place where pussies miaow no more,
She never noticed puss was stuffed;
Never mind, the old dears chuffed
And Morris's sincere attempt,
To show he, truly, did repent,
Were the first steps on his journey,
To qualify in Taxidermy.
Precocity can be alarming,
Though, to the human race, less harming,
As, thankfully, his skills applied,
To creatures who'd already died.
Both his parents, now less stressed,
Were overjoyed and they confessed
The pact they'd made was superseded;
A great big gooseberry bush was needed,

Under which they hoped to find,
Providing Mr. Stork was kind,
A sister for their little man
And, really, that's where we began.

Poet's Note:
Very few pussycats were damaged during research for this poem.

The Time Machine

Tick tick, tick tick, tick tick, tick tick;
Purposeful, familiar sound,
Smooth as clockwork, perfect timing,
Precision movement, fully wound.

Tick tick, tick tick, tick tick, tick tick;
Most accurate I've ever seen,
Predictable to half a second,
Regulated time machine.

Tick tick, tick tick, tick tick, tick tick;
Toenails on the tarmac road,
One more comfort break's in order,
Providing progress isn't slowed.

Tick tick, tick tick, tick tick, tick tick;
'Walkies' over, same old winner,
Dependable as Greenwich Meantime,
The dog who knows it's time for dinner!

Hippopotamus

The irascible hippopotamus,
If annoyed will undoubtedly harm us,
If you tickle its ear
Or poke sticks in its rear
Its reaction is bound to alarm us

Granny's metaphors often were rotten
But her wisdom I've never forgotten,
It wasn't a joke
When she said "never poke
A hippopotamus's bottom."

The unsavoury hippopotamus,
For its wind is enormously famous,
Its use is I fear,
When approaching its rear,
How the hippopotamus restrain us.

If you think that this rhyme doesn't scan,
It's all part of the poetic plan,
To sharpen the wits
So that every word fits,
Now read it again 'till you can.

The Message

The poet sat beneath a tree,
Puffing out his chest,
At his extraordinary talent,
This had to be the best,
The most magnificent, significant,
Poem ever written
In the history of the world;
With his creation he was smitten.

A pigeon flew from in its branches
And performed, as pigeons do,
A well-aimed criticism,
A ginormous pigeon-pooh!
The humbled poet pondered,
As on his verse the judgement spattered,
In the great big scheme of things,
His poem really hadn't mattered.

The End

If you're sad to reach the end
Because you've had such fun,
Don't forget without an end
You couldn't have begun.

I found a little bottle,
Hidden in a drawer,
In a cupboard in the attic
Where I'd never been before.
I was . . . .